Meatballs Recipes Cookbook

MARIA SOBININA

m-a-i-a.com & maiatea.com

MARIA SOBININA   m-a-i-a.com & maiatea.com

Copyright © 2019 - 2021 MARIA SOBININA
m-a-i-a.com & maiatea.com

All rights reserved.

ISBN- 9781676911111

DEDICATION

This book is dedicated to my beautiful family and friends, as well as to you, my reader. I am happy to share the amazing joy of cooking with you.

At m-a-i-a.com and MaiaTea.com we give back to the community. Every week we feed more than 100 people in need and provide them with the basic essentials. Sign up for our FREE recipes and stay tuned for our updates. cookbooks@m-a-i-a.com with Recipes in the subject.

TABLE OF CONTENTS

Italian Meatballs   9

Italian-American Meatballs   12

Swedish Meatballs   16

Turkish Meatballs   21

Spanish Meatballs   25

Mongolian Meatballs   29

Greek Meatballs   33

Mexican Meatballs   37

Thai Meatballs   40

Beef & Ricotta Meatballs   43

Barbeque Meatballs   47

Cranberry Meatballs   50

Red Curry Thai Meatballs   53

Beef & Mushrooms Meatballs   57

Beef, Beets & Mushrooms Meatballs   61

Turkey, Beets & Mushrooms Quinoa Meatballs   64

Lamb, Beets & Olives Meatballs   67

Beef, Broccoli & Olives Meatballs   70

Cauliflower & Chicken Meatballs   74

Salmon Meatballs   77

Chickpea Meatballs   80

Simple Beef & Pork Meatballs

Simple Beef & Pork Meatballs

INGREDIENTS:

8 Oz **Beef**, ground

8 Oz **Pork**, ground

¼ Cup **Milk,** whole

¼ Cup **Crumbs,** bread, white

1 **Egg,** large

½ Tablespoon **Italian Seasoning**

1 teaspoon **Salt,** fine, pink, Himalayan

Black Pepper, to taste

EQUIPMENT:

Small and Medium and large mixing bowls, Medium heat-proof pot, Large frying pan and/or Large baking tray, Measuring cups, Kitchen knife, Spatula.

DIRECTIONS:

Step 1: Place bread crumbs into a small mixing bowl and add warm milk. Mix well and leave on a countertop for ten to fifteen minutes.

Step 2: Place ground beef and ground pork into a medium mixing bowl.

Mix it well and add soften bread crumbs and egg to the mixture.

Step 3: Add spices, salt, and pepper and mix well to incorporate.

Step 4: Make round shape balls and place onto a large tray. Make sure the sides of the meatballs do not touch to ensure even cooking.

You can bake meatballs in an oven or fry them in a pan.

Bake the meatballs in an oven:

Step 1: Preheat the oven to 360°F.

Step 2: Place the tray with meatballs into the oven. Bake until meatballs internal temperature gets to 165°F. This can take between 50 minutes and 1 hour and ten minutes.

Fry the meatballs in a pan.

Step 1: Spray a frying pan with a cooking spray and preheat the pan. You can get away with not using cooking spray because there will be enough fat released during frying.

Step 2: Place the meatballs into the frying pan. Make sure the sides of meatballs do not touch to ensure an even cooking.

Fry for about 30 minutes, flipping from side to side, until meatballs internal temperature gets to 165°F.

Serve immediately.

Simple Beef & Pork Meatballs will keep for three days in a fridge or one month in a freezer.

Italian Meatballs

Italian Meatballs

INGREDIENTS:

1 Lbs. **Beef**, ground

½ Lbs. **Pork**, ground

½ Lbs. **Italian Sausage,** ground

½ Cup **Milk,** whole

1 Cup **Crumbs,** bread, white

½ Cup **Cheese**, parmesan, grated

2 **Eggs**, large

1 **Onion**, white, small, chopped

½ Cup **Parsley**, chopped

4 **Garlic Cloves**, finely minced

1 ½ Tablespoon **Olive Oil,** virgin, unrefined

½ Tablespoon **Italian Seasoning**

1 teaspoon **Salt,** fine, pink, Himalayan

Black Pepper, to taste

32 Oz **Marinara Sauce**

EQUIPMENT:

Small and Medium and large mixing bowls, Medium heat-proof pot, Large frying pan, Large baking tray, Measuring cups, Kitchen knife, Spatula.

DIRECTIONS:

Step 1: Place bread crumbs into a small mixing bowl and add warm milk. Mix well and leave on a countertop for ten to fifteen minutes.

Step 2: Place ground beef, ground pork and ground Italian sausage, onion, and garlic into a medium mixing bowl. Mix it well and add soften bread crumbs, eggs, parsley, parmesan cheese to the mixture.

Step 3: Add spices, salt, and pepper and mix well to incorporate.

Step 4: Make round shape balls and place onto a large tray. Make sure the sides of the meatballs do not touch to ensure even cooking. (baking)

Step 5: Sprinkle frying pan with oil. Sear meatballs for a few minutes.

You can bake meatballs in an oven or fry them in a pan.

Bake the meatballs in an oven:

Step 1: Preheat the oven to 360°F.

Step 2: Place seared meatballs into the tray. Add marinara sauce and place the tray with meatballs into the oven. Bake until meatballs internal temperature gets to 165°F. This can take between 50 minutes and 1 hour and ten minutes.

Cook the meatballs in a pan.

Step 1: Place the meatballs into a frying pan. Add marinara sauce.

Cook for about 30 minutes until meatballs internal temperature gets to 165°F.

Serve immediately.

Italian Meatballs will keep for three days in a fridge or one month in a freezer.

Italian-American Meatballs

INGREDIENTS:

¾ Lbs. **Beef**, ground

½ Lbs. **Pork**, ground

½ Lbs. **Veal,** ground

½ Cup **Milk,** whole

1 Cup **Crumbs,** bread, white

½ Cup **Cheese**, parmesan, grated

2 **Eggs**, large

1 **Onion**, white, small, chopped

½ Cup **Parsley**, chopped

4 **Garlic Cloves**, finely minced

1 ½ Tablespoon **Olive Oil,** virgin, unrefined

½ Tablespoon **Italian Seasoning**

1 teaspoon **Salt,** fine, pink, Himalayan

Black Pepper, to taste

32 Oz **Marinara Sauce**

EQUIPMENT:

Small and Medium and large mixing bowls, Medium heat-proof pot, Large frying pan, Large baking tray, Measuring cups, Kitchen knife, Spatula.

DIRECTIONS:

Step 1: Place bread crumbs into a small mixing bowl and add warm milk. Mix well and leave on a countertop for ten to fifteen minutes.

Step 2: Place ground beef, ground pork and ground veal, onion, and garlic into a medium mixing bowl. Mix it well and add soften bread crumbs, eggs, parsley, parmesan cheese to the mixture.

Step 3: Add spices, salt, and pepper and mix well to incorporate.

Step 4: Make round shape balls and place onto a large tray. Make sure the sides of the meatballs do not touch to ensure even cooking. (baking)

Step 5: Sprinkle frying pan with oil. Sear meatballs for a few minutes.

You can bake meatballs in an oven or fry them in a pan.

Bake the meatballs in an oven:

Step 1: Preheat the oven to 360°F.

Step 2: Place seared meatballs into the tray. Add marinara sauce and place the tray with meatballs into the oven. Bake until meatballs internal temperature gets to 165°F. This can take between 50 minutes and 1 hour and ten minutes.

Cook the meatballs in a pan.

Step 1: Place the meatballs into a frying pan. Add marinara sauce.

Cook for about 30 minutes until meatballs internal temperature gets to 165°F.

Serve immediately.

Italian-American Meatballs will keep for three days in a fridge or one month in a freezer.

Swedish Meatballs

Swedish Meatballs

INGREDIENTS:

FOR THE MEATBALLS:

1 Lbs. **Chicken**, ground

½ Lbs. **Beef**, ground

½ Cup **Milk,** whole

1 Cup **Crumbs,** bread, white

2 **Eggs**, large

½ Cup **Parsley**, chopped

3 **Garlic Cloves**, finely minced

1 ½ Tablespoon **Olive Oil,** virgin, unrefined

½ Tablespoon **Allspice**

1 teaspoon **Salt,** fine, pink, Himalayan

Black Pepper, to taste

FOR THE SAUCE:

2 Cups **Sour Cream**, full fat

½ Cup **Flour**, all-purpose

1 teaspoon **Dijon mustard**

4 Tablespoons **Butter**

½ teaspoon **Rosemary**, dried

½ teaspoon **Sage**, dried

½ teaspoon **Garlic**, powder

EQUIPMENT:

Small and Medium and large mixing bowls, Medium heat-proof pot, Large frying pan, Large baking tray, Measuring cups, Kitchen knife, Spatula.

DIRECTIONS:

MAKE THE MEATBALLS:

Step 1: Place bread crumbs into a small mixing bowl and add warm milk. Mix well and leave on a countertop for ten to fifteen minutes.

Step 2: Place ground beef, ground chicken and garlic into a medium mixing bowl. Mix it well and add soften bread crumbs, eggs, and parsley to the mixture.

Step 3: Add spices, salt, and pepper and mix well to incorporate.

Step 4: Make round shape balls and place onto a large tray. Make sure the sides of the meatballs do not touch to ensure even cooking. (baking)

Step 5: Sprinkle frying pan with oil. Sear meatballs for a few minutes.

You can bake meatballs in an oven or fry them in a pan.

Bake the meatballs in an oven:

Step 1: Preheat the oven to 360°F.

Step 2: Place seared meatballs into the tray. Add marinara sauce and place the tray with meatballs into the oven. Bake until meatballs internal temperature gets to 165°F. This can take between 50 minutes and 1 hour and ten minutes.

Cook the meatballs in a pan.

Step 1: Place the meatballs into a frying pan. Add marinara sauce.

Cook for about 30 minutes until meatballs internal temperature gets to 165°F.

While meatballs are cooking, prepare the sauce.

MAKE THE SAUCE:

Step 1: Place the butter into a pre-heat skillet. Melt the butter and add the flour to the butter periodically stirring.

Step 2: Add sour cream and cook the sauce for 5-7 minutes. Add spices and salt and cook for another minute.

Serve immediately.

Swedish Meatballs will keep for three days in a fridge or one month in a freezer.

MARIA SOBININA   m-a-i-a.com & maiatea.com

Turkish Meatballs

Turkish Meatballs

INGREDIENTS:

1 Lbs. **Lamb**, ground

1 Lbs. **Beef**, ground

½ Cup **Milk,** whole

1 Cup **Crumbs,** bread, white

2 **Eggs**, large

3 **Garlic Cloves**, finely minced

1 Tablespoon **Lemon**, juice

1 ½ Tablespoon **Olive Oil,** virgin, unrefined

1 teaspoon Cumin, ground

1 teaspoon Pepper, black, ground

1 teaspoon Pepper, red, flakes

1 teaspoon Thyme, dried

2 teaspoons **Salt,** fine, pink, Himalayan

EQUIPMENT:

Small and Medium and large mixing bowls, Medium heat-proof pot, Large frying pan, Large baking tray, Measuring cups, Kitchen knife, Spatula.

DIRECTIONS:

MAKE THE MEATBALLS:

Step 1: Place bread crumbs into a small mixing bowl and add warm milk. Mix well and leave on a countertop for ten to fifteen minutes.

Step 2: Place ground beef, ground lamb and garlic into a medium mixing bowl. Mix it well and add soften bread crumbs, eggs, and lemon juice to the mixture.

Step 3: Add spices, salt, and pepper and mix well to incorporate.

Step 4: Make round shape balls and place onto a large tray. Make sure the sides of the meatballs do not touch to ensure even cooking. (baking)

Step 5: Sprinkle frying pan with oil. Sear meatballs for a few minutes.

You can bake meatballs in an oven or fry them in a pan.

Bake the meatballs in an oven:

Step 1: Preheat the oven to 360°F.

Step 2: Place seared meatballs into the tray. Add marinara sauce and place the tray with meatballs into the oven. Bake until meatballs internal temperature gets to 165°F. This can take between 50 minutes and 1 hour and ten minutes.

Cook the meatballs in a pan.

Place the meatballs into a frying pan. Add marinara sauce.

Cook for about 30 minutes until meatballs internal temperature gets to 165°F.

While meatballs are cooking, prepare the sauce.

Serve immediately.

Turkish Meatballs will keep for three days in a fridge or one month in a freezer.

Spanish Meatballs

SPANISH MEATBALLS

INGREDIENTS:

FOR THE MEATBALLS:

1 Lbs. **Beef**, ground

1 Lbs. **Pork**, ground

½ Cup **Prosciutto,** finely minced

½ Cup **Milk,** whole

1 Cup **Crumbs,** bread, white

½ Cup **Cheese**, parmesan, grated

1 **Egg**, large

½ Cup **Onion**, white, finely minced

½ Cup **Parsley**, chopped

4 **Garlic Cloves**, finely minced

1 ½ Tablespoon **Olive Oil,** virgin, unrefined

½ teaspoon **Paprika,** ground

1 teaspoon **Salt,** fine, pink, Himalayan

Black Pepper, to taste

FOR THE SAUCE:

1 Can **Tomatoes,** whole, pureed

¾ Cup **Onion**, white, finely chopped

½ Cup **Parsley**, chopped

½ Cup **Chicken Broth**

1/3 Cup **Wine**, white, dry

½ Cup **Olive Oil**, virgin, cold pressed

½ teaspoon **Paprika,** ground

¼ teaspoon **Red Chili Flakes**

1 teaspoon **Salt,** fine, pink, Himalayan

EQUIPMENT:

Small and Medium and large mixing bowls, Medium heat-proof pot, Large frying pan, Large baking tray, Measuring cups, Kitchen knife, Spatula.

DIRECTIONS:

MAKE THE MEATBALLS:

Step 1: Place bread crumbs into a small mixing bowl and add warm milk. Mix well and leave on a countertop for ten to fifteen minutes.

Step 2: Place ground beef, ground pork and finely minced prosciutto, onion, and garlic into a medium mixing bowl. Mix it well and add soften bread crumbs, eggs, parsley, parmesan cheese to the mixture.

Step 3: Add spices, salt, and pepper and mix well to incorporate.

Step 4: Make round shape balls and place onto a large tray. Make sure the sides of the meatballs do not touch to ensure even cooking. (baking)

Step 5: Sprinkle frying pan with oil. Sear meatballs for a few minutes.

You can bake meatballs in an oven or fry them in a pan.

Bake the meatballs in an oven:

Step 1: Preheat the oven to 360°F.

Step 2: Place seared meatballs into the tray. Add marinara sauce and place the tray with meatballs into the oven. Bake until meatballs internal temperature gets to 165°F. This can take between 50 minutes and 1 hour and ten minutes.

Cook the meatballs in a pan.

Place the meatballs into a frying pan. Add marinara sauce.

Cook for about 30 minutes until meatballs internal temperature gets to 165°F.

MAKE THE SAUCE:

Step 1: Place the olive oil into a pre-heated skillet. Add the onion and sauté it for a few minutes until it becomes soft.

Step 2: Add spices, salt, and wine and cook for another 20 – 30 seconds. Add tomatoes and simmer for 7-10 minutes.

Serve immediately.

Spanish Meatballs will keep for three days in a fridge or one month in a freezer.

Mongolian Meatballs

INGREDIENTS:

1 ½ Lbs. **Beef**, ground

¼ Cup **Crumbs,** panko bread

1 **Egg**, large

½ Cup **Broth**, chicken

¼ Cup **Soy Sauce**, low sodium

¼ Cup **Sugar**, brown

2 Cloves, **Garlic**, finely minced

½ **Ginger**, finely minced

3 **Onions**, green, thinly sliced, separated in two halves

2 Tablespoons, **Hoisin Sauce**

2 teaspoons **Sesame Oil**, separated in two halves

½ Tablespoon **Italian Seasoning**

1 teaspoon **Salt,** fine, pink, Himalayan

¼ teaspoon **Red Pepper**, flakes

Black Pepper, to taste

Sesame seeds for garnish

EQUIPMENT:

Small and Medium and large mixing bowls, Medium heat-proof pot, Large frying pan and/or Large baking tray, Measuring cups, Kitchen knife, Spatula.

DIRECTIONS:

MAKE THE SAUCE:

Add one teaspoon of sesame oil onto a pre-heated pan. Stir in ginger and simmer for about 30 seconds, constantly stirring. Add brown sugar, salt, chicken broth, soy sauce, and hoisin sauce. Cook for about 5 minutes.

MAKE THE MEATBALLS:

Step 1: Place ground beef, panko bread crumbs, one half of the green onions, one teaspoon of sesame oil into a medium mixing bowl. Mix well.

Step 2: Add spices, garlic (excluding ginger) and mix again to incorporate.

Form the meatballs.

You can bake meatballs in an oven or fry them in a pan.

Bake the meatballs in an oven:

Step 1: Preheat the oven to 360°F.

Spray a large skillet with a cooking spread. Place meatballs into the skillet and sear for a few minutes on each side until there is a brown crust. Transfer the meatballs into the baking tray.

Step 2: Place the tray with meatballs into the oven. Bake for 25 minutes, add the sauce 25 minutes into baking. Bake until meatballs internal temperature gets to 165°F. This can take between 50 minutes and 1 hour and ten minutes.

Garnish with the remailing green onions.

Fry the meatballs in a pan.

Step 1: Spray a frying pan with a cooking spray and preheat the pan. Place meatballs into the skillet and sear for a few minutes on each side until there is a brown crust.

Step 2: Fry the meatballs for about 15 minutes, flipping from side to side, add the sauce, and cook for another 15 minutes, until meatballs' internal temperature gets to 165°F.

Garnish with the remailing green onions.

Serve immediately.

Mongolian Meatballs will keep for three days in a fridge or one month in a freezer.

Greek Meatballs

INGREDIENTS:

FOR THE MEATBALLS:

1 ½ Lbs. **Beef**, ground

½ Lbs. **Lamb,** ground

¼ Cup **Crumbs,** panko bread

1 **Egg,** large

2 Oz **Feta Cheese**, crumbled

½ Cup **Parsley**, chopped

2 Cloves, **Garlic**, finely minced

2 Tablespoons **Lemon**, juice

1 teaspoon **Oregano**, dried

1 teaspoon **Cumin**, ground

1 teaspoon **Salt**, fine, pink, Himalayan

Black Pepper, to taste

FOR THE TZATZIKI SAUCE:

1 Cup **Cucumber**, shredded

2 Cups **Yogurt**, Greek, plain

½ **Lemon**, Juice

¼ Cup **Dill**, finely chopped

1 Clove, **Garlic**, finely minced

EQUIPMENT:

Small and Medium and large mixing bowls, Medium heat-proof pot, Large frying pan and/or Large baking tray, Measuring cups, Kitchen knife, Spatula.

DIRECTIONS:

Step 1: Place ground beef and ground lamb into a medium mixing bowl. Mix it well

Step 2: Add lemon juice, bread crumbs, feta cheese, egg, spices, and salt to the mixture.

Step 3: Make round shape balls and place onto a large tray. Make sure the sides of the meatballs do not touch to ensure even cooking.

Step 4: Preheat the oven to 360°F.

Step 5: Place the tray with meatballs into the oven. Bake until meatballs internal temperature gets to 165°F.

MAKE THE SAUCE:

In a medium bowl, combine all ingredients. Whisk until all is incorporated.

Serve immediately. Deep the meatballs into the sauce.

Greek Meatballs will keep for three days in a fridge or one month in a freezer.

MARIA SOBININA   m-a-i-a.com & maiatea.com

Mexican Meatballs

Mexican Meatballs

INGREDIENTS:

1 Lbs. **Beef**, ground

1 Lbs. **Pork**, ground

½ Cup **Rice**, pre-cooked (should be a little hard)

½ Cup **Cheese**, parmesan, grated

2 **Eggs**, large

1 **Onion**, white, small, chopped

½ Cup **Parsley**, chopped

4 **Garlic Cloves**, finely minced

1 ½ Tablespoon **Olive Oil,** virgin, unrefined

1 tsp ground cumin

1 tsp ground oregano

1 tsp ground paprika1 teaspoon **Salt,** fine, pink, Himalayan

Black Pepper, to taste

32 Oz **Marinara Sauce**

EQUIPMENT:

Small and Medium and large mixing bowls, Medium heat-proof pot, Large frying pan, Large baking tray, Measuring cups, Kitchen knife, Spatula.

DIRECTIONS:

Step 1: Place ground beef, ground pork, onion, and garlic into a medium mixing bowl. Mix it well and add rice, eggs, parsley, parmesan cheese to the mixture.

Step 2: Add spices, salt, and pepper and mix well to incorporate.

Step 3: Make round shape balls and place onto a large tray. Make sure the sides of the meatballs do not touch to ensure even cooking. (baking)

Step 4: Sprinkle frying pan with oil. Sear meatballs for a few minutes.

You can bake meatballs in an oven or fry them in a pan.

Bake the meatballs in an oven:

Step 1: Preheat the oven to 360°F.

Step 2: Place seared meatballs into the tray. Add marinara sauce and place the tray with meatballs into the oven. Bake until meatballs internal temperature gets to 165°F. This can take between 50 minutes and 1 hour and ten minutes.

Cook the meatballs in a pan.

Step 1: Place the meatballs into a frying pan. Add marinara sauce.

Cook for about 30 minutes until meatballs internal temperature gets to 165°F.

Serve immediately.

Mexican Meatballs will keep for three days in a fridge or one month in a freezer.

Thai Meatballs

INGREDIENTS:

FOR THE MEATBALLS:

1 ½ Lbs. **Chicken**, ground

½ Cup **Crumbs,** panko bread

1 **Egg**, large

½ Cup **Parsley**, chopped

3 Cloves **Garlic**, finely grated

1 Tablespoon **Thai Red Curry**, paste

1 Tablespoon **Fish Sauce**

2 **Scallions**, finely chopped

1 **Jalapeno**, large, finely chopped

1 Tablespoon **Lemongrass**, finely chopped

1 Tablespoon **Cilantro**, chopped

1 teaspoon **Salt**, fine, pink, Himalayan

Black Pepper, to taste

FOR THE SAUCE:

1 Cup **Thai Chili Sauce**, sweet

1 Tablespoon **Soy Sauce**

1 Tablespoon **Wine Vinegar**

½ **Lime**, juice

1 Clove, **Garlic**, finely minced

EQUIPMENT:

Small and Medium and large mixing bowls, Medium heat-proof pot, Large frying pan and/or Large baking tray, Measuring cups, Kitchen knife, Spatula.

DIRECTIONS:

Step 1: Place ground beef and ground lamb into a medium mixing bowl. Mix it well

Step 2: Add lemon juice, bread crumbs, feta cheese, egg, spices, and salt to the mixture.

Step 3: Make round shape balls and place onto a large tray. Make sure the sides of the meatballs do not touch to ensure even cooking.

Step 4: Preheat the oven to 360°F.

Step 5: Place the tray with meatballs into the oven. Bake until meatballs internal temperature gets to 165°F.

MAKE THE SAUCE:

In a medium bowl, combine all ingredients. Whisk until all is incorporated.

Serve immediately. Deep the meatballs into the sauce or cover the meatballs with the sauce.

Thai Meatballs will keep for three days in a fridge or one month in a freezer.

BEEF & RICOTTA MEATBALLS

INGREDIENTS:

16 Oz **Beef**, ground

8 Oz **Ricotta Cheese**

¼ Cup **Milk,** whole

¼ Cup **Crumbs,** bread, white

1 **Egg**, large

1 Clove **Garlic**, grated

½ Tablespoon **Italian Seasoning**

1 teaspoon **Salt,** fine, pink, Himalayan

Black Pepper, to taste

EQUIPMENT:

Small and Medium and large mixing bowls, Medium heat-proof pot, Large frying pan and/or Large baking tray, Measuring cups, Kitchen knife, Spatula.

DIRECTIONS:

Step 1: Place bread crumbs into a small mixing bowl and add warm milk. Mix well and leave on a countertop for ten to fifteen minutes.

Step 2: Place ground beef and ricotta cheese into a medium mixing bowl. Mix it well and add soften bread crumbs and egg to the mixture.

Step 3: Add garlic, spices, salt, and pepper and mix well to incorporate.

Step 4: Make round shape balls and place onto a large tray. Make sure the sides of the meatballs do not touch to ensure even cooking.

You can bake meatballs in an oven or fry them in a pan.

Bake the meatballs in an oven:

Step 1: Preheat the oven to 360°F.

Step 2: Place the tray with meatballs into the oven. Bake until meatballs internal temperature gets to 165°F. This can take between 50 minutes and 1 hour and ten minutes.

Fry the meatballs in a pan.

Step 1: Spray a frying pan with a cooking spray and preheat the pan. You can get away with not using cooking spray because there will be enough fat released during frying.

Step 2: Place the meatballs into the frying pan. Make sure the sides of meatballs do not touch to ensure an even cooking.

Fry for about 30 minutes, flipping from side to side, until meatballs internal temperature gets to 165°F.

Serve immediately.

Beef & Ricotta Meatballs will keep for three days in a fridge or one month in a freezer.

Barbeque Meatballs

BARBEQUE MEATBALLS

INGREDIENTS:

16 Oz **Beef**, ground

¼ Cup **Milk,** whole

¼ Cup **Crumbs,** bread, white

1 **Egg**, large

½ Tablespoon **Italian Seasoning**

1 teaspoon **Salt,** fine, pink, Himalayan

Black Pepper, to taste

18 Oz **Barbeque Sauce**

EQUIPMENT:

Small and Medium and large mixing bowls, Medium heat-proof pot, Large frying pan and/or Large baking tray, Measuring cups, Kitchen knife, Spatula.

DIRECTIONS:

Step 1: Place bread crumbs into a small mixing bowl and add warm milk. Mix well and leave on a countertop for ten to fifteen minutes.

Step 2: Place ground beef and ground pork into a medium mixing bowl. Mix it well and add soften bread crumbs and egg to the mixture.

Step 3: Add spices, salt, and pepper and mix well to incorporate.

Step 4: Make round shape balls and place onto a large tray. Make sure the sides of the meatballs do not touch to ensure even cooking.

Bake the meatballs in an oven:

Step 1: Preheat the oven to 360°F.

Step 2: Place the tray with meatballs into the oven. Bake until meatballs internal temperature gets to 165°F. This can take between 50 minutes and 1 hour and ten minutes. Thirty minutes into baking add barbeque sauce over the meatballs.

Serve immediately.

Barbeque Meatballs will keep for three days in a fridge or one month in a freezer.

Cranberry Meatballs

Cranberry Meatballs

INGREDIENTS:

16 Oz **Beef**, ground

½ Cup **Coconut Flour**

1 **Egg**, large

½ Tablespoon **Italian Seasoning**

1 teaspoon **Salt**, fine, pink, Himalayan

Black Pepper, to taste

1 Can **Cranberry Sauce**

½ Cup **Barbeque Sauce**

EQUIPMENT:

Small and Medium and large mixing bowls, Medium heat-proof pot, Large frying pan and/or Large baking tray, Measuring cups, Kitchen knife, Spatula.

DIRECTIONS:

Step 1: Place bread crumbs into a small mixing bowl and add warm milk. Mix well and leave on a countertop for ten to fifteen minutes.

Step 2: Place ground beef into a medium mixing bowl. Mix it well and add coconut flour and egg to the mixture.

Step 3: Add spices, salt, and pepper and mix well to incorporate.

Step 4: Make round shape balls and place onto a large tray. Make sure the sides of the meatballs do not touch to ensure even cooking.

Make the Sauce:

In a medium mixing bowl combine cranberry cause and barbeque sauce.

Bake the meatballs in an oven:

Step 1: Preheat the oven to 360°F.

Step 2: Place the tray with meatballs into the oven. Bake until meatballs internal temperature gets to 165°F. This can take between 50 minutes and 1 hour and ten minutes. Thirty minutes into baking add barbeque sauce over the meatballs.

Serve immediately.

Cranberry Meatballs will keep for three days in a fridge or one month in a freezer.

Red Curry Thai Meatballs

Red Curry Thai Meatballs

INGREDIENTS:

FOR THE MEATBALLS:

2 Lbs. **Turkey**, ground

1 **Onion**, white, finely minced

1 Cup **Crumbs,** bread, white

2 **Eggs**, large

½ Cup **Parsley**, chopped

1 Tablespoon **Ginger**, ground

4 **Garlic Cloves**, finely minced

1 ½ Tablespoon **Olive Oil,** virgin, unrefined

½ teaspoon **Paprika,** ground

1 teaspoon **Salt,** fine, pink, Himalayan

Black Pepper, to taste

FOR THE SAUCE:

1 Cup **Chicken Broth**

1 Cup **Onion**, white, finely chopped

3/4 Cup **Peanut Butter**, smooth

1 Inch **Ginger**, finely grated

4 **Garlic Cloves**, finely minced

3 Tablespoon **Red Curry**, paste

½ Cup **Cilantro**, chopped

2 Tablespoons **Coconut Oil**, virgin, cold pressed

¼ teaspoon **Red Chili Flakes**

1 teaspoon **Salt,** fine, pink, Himalayan

EQUIPMENT:

Small and Medium and large mixing bowls, Medium heat-proof pot, Large frying pan, Large baking tray, Measuring cups, Kitchen knife, Spatula.

DIRECTIONS:

MAKE THE MEATBALLS:

Step 1: Place ground turkey, onion, ginger, and garlic into a medium mixing bowl. Mix it well and add bread crumbs, eggs, parsley to the mixture.

Step 2: Add spices, salt, and pepper and mix well to incorporate.

Step 3: Make round shape balls and place onto a large tray. Make sure the sides of the meatballs do not touch to ensure even cooking. (baking)

Step 4: Sprinkle frying pan with oil. Sear meatballs for a few minutes.

You can bake meatballs in an oven or fry them in a pan.

Bake the meatballs in an oven:

Step 1: Preheat the oven to 360°F.

Step 2: Place seared meatballs into the tray. Add marinara sauce and place the tray with meatballs into the oven. Bake until meatballs internal temperature gets to 165°F. This can take between 50 minutes and 1 hour and ten minutes.

Cook the meatballs in a pan.

Step 1: Place the meatballs into a frying pan. Add marinara sauce.

Cook for about 30 minutes until meatballs internal temperature gets to 165°F.

MAKE THE SAUCE:

Step 1: Place the coconut oil into a pre-heat skillet.

Add the onion and sauté it for a few minutes until it becomes soft.

Step 2: Add spices, garlic, ginger, salt, and chicken broth and cook for another 2-3 minutes. Add peanut butter and cook for another few minutes.

Serve immediately.

Red Curry Thai Meatballs will keep for three days in a fridge or one month in a freezer.

Beef & Mushrooms Meatballs

INGREDIENTS:

1 Lbs. **Beef**, ground

8 Oz **Mushrooms**, raw, white, chopped

¼ Cup **Milk,** whole

¼ Cup **Crumbs,** bread, white

1 **Egg**, large

½ Tablespoon **Italian Seasoning**

1 teaspoon **Salt,** fine, pink, Himalayan

Black Pepper, to taste

EQUIPMENT:

Small and Medium and large mixing bowls, Medium heat-proof pot, Large frying pan and/or Large baking tray, Measuring cups, Kitchen knife, Spatula.

DIRECTIONS:

Step 1: Place bread crumbs into a small mixing bowl and add warm milk. Mix well and leave on a countertop for ten to fifteen minutes.

Step 2: Place ground beef and chopped mushrooms into a medium mixing bowl. Mix it well and add soften bread crumbs and egg to the mixture.

Step 3: Add spices, salt, and pepper and mix well to incorporate.

Step 4: Make round shape balls and place onto a large tray. Make sure the sides of the meatballs do not touch to ensure even cooking.

You can bake meatballs in an oven or fry them in a pan.

Bake the meatballs in an oven:

Step 1: Preheat the oven to 360°F.

Step 2: Place the tray with meatballs into the oven. Bake until meatballs internal temperature gets to 165°F. This can take between 50 minutes and 1 hour and ten minutes.

Fry the meatballs in a pan.

Step 1: Spray a frying pan with a cooking spray and preheat the pan. You can get away with not using cooking spray because there will be enough fat released during frying.

Step 2: Place the meatballs into the frying pan. Make sure the sides of meatballs do not touch to ensure an even cooking.

Fry for about 30 minutes, flipping from side to side, until meatballs internal temperature gets to 165°F.

Serve immediately.

Beef & Mushrooms Meatballs will keep for three days in a fridge or one month in a freezer.

Beef, Beets & Mushrooms Meatballs

Beef, Beets & Mushrooms Meatballs

INGREDIENTS:

1 Lbs. **Beef**, ground

8 Oz **Mushrooms**, raw, white, chopped

8 Oz **Beets**, cooked, grated

¼ Cup **Milk,** whole

¼ Cup **Crumbs,** bread, white

1 **Egg**, large

½ Tablespoon **Italian Seasoning**

1 teaspoon **Salt,** fine, pink, Himalayan

Black Pepper, to taste

EQUIPMENT:

Small and Medium and large mixing bowls, Medium heat-proof pot, Large frying pan and/or Large baking tray, Grater, Measuring cups, Kitchen knife, Spatula.

DIRECTIONS:

Step 1: Place bread crumbs into a small mixing bowl and add warm milk. Mix well and leave on a countertop for ten to fifteen minutes.

Step 2: Place ground beef, grated beets, and chopped mushrooms into a medium mixing bowl. Mix it well and add soften bread crumbs and egg to the mixture.

Step 3: Add spices, salt, and pepper and mix well to incorporate.

Step 4: Make round shape balls and place onto a large tray. Make sure the sides of the meatballs do not touch to ensure even cooking.

You can bake meatballs in an oven or fry them in a pan.

Bake the meatballs in an oven:

Step 1: Preheat the oven to 360°F.

Step 2: Place the tray with meatballs into the oven. Bake until meatballs internal temperature gets to 165°F. This can take between 50 minutes and 1 hour and ten minutes.

Fry the meatballs in a pan.

Step 1: Spray a frying pan with a cooking spray and preheat the pan. You can get away with not using cooking spray because there will be enough fat released during frying.

Step 2: Place the meatballs into the frying pan. Make sure the sides of meatballs do not touch to ensure an even cooking.

Fry for about 30 minutes, flipping from side to side, until meatballs internal temperature gets to 165°F.

Serve immediately.

Beef, Beets & Mushrooms Meatballs will keep for three days in a fridge or one month in a freezer.

Turkey, Beets & Mushrooms Quinoa Meatballs

INGREDIENTS:

1 Lbs. **Turkey**, ground

8 Oz **Mushrooms**, raw, white, chopped

8 Oz **Beets**, cooked, grated

1 Cup **Quinoa**, pre-cooked

½ Cup **Coconut Flour**

½ Tablespoon **Italian Seasoning**

1 teaspoon **Salt,** fine, pink, Himalayan

Black Pepper, to taste

EQUIPMENT:

Small and Medium and large mixing bowls, Medium heat-proof pot, Large frying pan and/or Large baking tray, Grater, Measuring cups, Kitchen knife, Spatula.

DIRECTIONS:

Cook and grate beets. Cook and drain quinoa.

Step 1: Place ground turkey, grated beets, and chopped mushrooms into a medium mixing bowl. Mix it well and add cooked quinoa and coconut flour to the mixture.

Step 2: Add spices, salt, and pepper and mix well to incorporate.

Step 3: Make round shape balls and place onto a large tray. Make sure the sides of the meatballs do not touch to ensure even cooking.

You can bake meatballs in an oven or fry them in a pan.

Bake the meatballs in an oven:

Step 1: Preheat the oven to 360°F.

Step 2: Place the tray with meatballs into the oven. Bake until meatballs internal temperature gets to 165°F. This can take between 50 minutes and 1 hour and ten minutes.

Fry the meatballs in a pan.

Step 1: Spray a frying pan with a cooking spray and preheat the pan. You can get away with not using cooking spray because there will be enough fat released during frying.

Step 2: Place the meatballs into the frying pan. Make sure the sides of meatballs do not touch to ensure an even cooking.

Fry for about 30 minutes, flipping from side to side, until meatballs internal temperature gets to 165°F.

Serve immediately.

Turkey, Beets & Mushrooms Quinoa Meatballs will keep for three days in a fridge or one month in a freezer.

Lamb, Beets & Olives Meatballs

INGREDIENTS:

1 Lbs. **Lamb**, ground

1 Can **Olives**, black, pitted

8 Oz **Beets**, cooked, grated

1 Cup **Coconut Flour**

1 teaspoon **Salt,** fine, pink, Himalayan

Black Pepper, to taste

EQUIPMENT:

Small and Medium and large mixing bowls, Medium heat-proof pot, Large frying pan and/or Large baking tray, Grater, Measuring cups, Kitchen knife, Spatula.

DIRECTIONS:

Cook and grate beets. Process pitted olives in a food processor until smooth.

Step 1: Place ground lamb, grated beets, and olives into a medium mixing bowl. Mix it well and add coconut flour to the mixture.

Step 2: Add spices, salt, and pepper and mix well to incorporate.

Step 3: Make round shape balls and place onto a large tray. Make sure the sides of the meatballs do not touch to ensure even cooking.

You can bake meatballs in an oven or fry them in a pan.

Bake the meatballs in an oven:

Step 1: Preheat the oven to 360°F.

Step 2: Place the tray with meatballs into the oven. Bake until meatballs internal temperature gets to 165°F. This can take between 50 minutes and 1 hour and ten minutes.

Fry the meatballs in a pan.

Step 1: Spray a frying pan with a cooking spray and preheat the pan. You can get away with not using cooking spray because there will be enough fat released during frying.

Step 2: Place the meatballs into the frying pan. Make sure the sides of meatballs do not touch to ensure an even cooking.

Fry for about 30 minutes, flipping from side to side, until meatballs internal temperature gets to 165°F.

Serve immediately.

Lamb, Beets & Olives Meatballs will keep for three days in a fridge or one month in a freezer.

Beef, Broccoli & Olives Meatballs

INGREDIENTS:

1 Lbs. **Beef**, ground

1 Can **Olives**, black, pitted

8 Oz **Broccoli**, cooked, grated

½ Cup **Coconut Flour**

½ Cup **Oatmeal Flour**

1 teaspoon **Salt,** fine, pink, Himalayan

Black Pepper, to taste

EQUIPMENT:

Small and Medium and large mixing bowls, Medium heat-proof pot, Large frying pan and/or Large baking tray, Grater, Measuring cups, Kitchen knife, Spatula.

DIRECTIONS:

Cook and grate broccoli. Process pitted olives in a food processor until smooth.

Step 1: Place ground beef, grated broccoli, and olives into a medium mixing bowl. Mix it well and add oatmeal flour and coconut flour to the mixture.

Step 2: Add spices, salt, and pepper and mix well to incorporate.

Step 3: Make round shape balls and place onto a large tray. Make sure the sides of the meatballs do not touch to ensure even cooking.

You can bake meatballs in an oven or fry them in a pan.

Bake the meatballs in an oven:

Step 1: Preheat the oven to 360°F.

Step 2: Place the tray with meatballs into the oven. Bake until meatballs internal temperature gets to 165°F. This can take between 50 minutes and 1 hour and ten minutes.

Fry the meatballs in a pan.

Step 1: Spray a frying pan with a cooking spray and preheat the pan. You can get away with not using cooking spray because there will be enough fat released during frying.

Step 2: Place the meatballs into the frying pan. Make sure the sides of meatballs do not touch to ensure an even cooking.

Fry for about 30 minutes, flipping from side to side, until meatballs internal temperature gets to 165°F.

Serve immediately.

Beef, Broccoli & Olives Meatballs will keep for three days in a fridge or one month in a freezer.

Cauliflower & Chicken Meatballs

Cauliflower & Chicken Meatballs

INGREDIENTS:

1 Lbs. **Chicken**, ground

10 Oz **Cauliflower**, boiled (soft), grated

¼ Cup **Milk,** whole

¼ Cup **Crumbs,** bread, white

1 **Egg,** large

½ Tablespoon **Italian Seasoning**

1 teaspoon **Salt,** fine, pink, Himalayan

Black Pepper, to taste

EQUIPMENT:

Small and Medium and large mixing bowls, Medium heat-proof pot, Large frying pan and/or Large baking tray, Measuring cups, Kitchen knife, Spatula.

DIRECTIONS:

Step 1: Place bread crumbs into a small mixing bowl and add warm milk. Mix well and leave on a countertop for ten to fifteen minutes.

Step 2: Place ground chicken and grated cauliflower into a medium mixing bowl. Mix it well and add soften bread crumbs and egg to the mixture.

Step 3: Add spices, salt, and pepper and mix well to incorporate.

Step 4: Make round shape balls and place onto a large tray. Make sure the sides of the meatballs do not touch to ensure even cooking.

You can bake meatballs in an oven or fry them in a pan.

Bake the meatballs in an oven:

Step 1: Preheat the oven to 360°F.

Step 2: Place the tray with meatballs into the oven. Bake until meatballs internal temperature gets to 165°F. This can take between 50 minutes and 1 hour and ten minutes.

Fry the meatballs in a pan.

Step 1: Spray a frying pan with a cooking spray and preheat the pan. You can get away with not using cooking spray because there will be enough fat released during frying.

Step 2: Place the meatballs into the frying pan. Make sure the sides of meatballs do not touch to ensure an even cooking.

Fry for about 30 minutes, flipping from side to side, until meatballs internal temperature gets to 165°F.

Serve immediately.

Beef & Mushrooms Meatballs will keep for three days in a fridge or one month in a freezer.

Salmon Meatballs

INGREDIENTS:

1 Lbs. **Salmon**, skinless

½ Cup **Bread**, crumbs

½ Cup **Cilantro**, finely chopped

1 **Egg**, large

½ Tablespoon **Italian Seasoning**

1 teaspoon **Salt**, fine, pink, Himalayan

Black Pepper, to taste

FOR THE SAUCE:

1 Cup **Cashews**, soaked

1 **Avocado**, peeled, pitted

½ Clove **Garlic**, minced

½ inch **Ginger**, root, peeled

½ **Lime**, juice of

¼ Cup **Cilantro**, chopped

1 teaspoon **Salt**, fine, pink, Himalayan

EQUIPMENT:

Small and Medium and large mixing bowls, Medium heat-proof pot, Large frying pan and/or Large baking tray, Measuring cups, Kitchen knife, Spatula.

DIRECTIONS:

Step 1: Place salmon into a food processor and pulse to chop it.

Step 2: Transfer chopped salmon into a medium mixing bowl, add bread crumbs, and egg and mix it well.

Step 3: Add spices, salt, and pepper and mix well to incorporate.

Step 4: Make round shape balls and place onto a large tray. Make sure the sides of the meatballs do not touch to ensure even cooking.

You can bake meatballs in an oven or fry them in a pan.

Bake the meatballs in an oven:

Step 1: Preheat the oven to 360°F.

Step 2: Place the tray with meatballs into the oven. Bake meatballs for 15-20 minutes.

Fry the meatballs in a pan.

Step 1: Spray a frying pan with a cooking spray and preheat the pan. You can get away with not using cooking spray because there will be enough fat released during frying.

Step 2: Place the meatballs into the frying pan. Make sure the sides of meatballs do not touch to ensure an even cooking.

Fry for about 15 minutes, flipping from side to side.

MAKE THE SAUCE:

Soak cashews for a few hours or overnight.

In a food processor combine soaked cashews, avocado, garlic, ginger, lime juice, cilantro, salt and pepper. Process until smooth.

Serve immediately.

Salmon Meatballs will keep for three days in a fridge or one month in a freezer.

Chickpea Meatballs

INGREDIENTS:

2 Cans **Chickpeas**

1 ½ Cups **Rice**, brown, cooked

½ Cup **Coconut Flour**

4 **Garlic**, cloves, peeled

2 Tablespoons **Olive Oil**, virgin, cold pressed

½ Tablespoon **Italian Seasoning**

1 teaspoon **Oregano**, dried

1 teaspoon **Salt,** fine, pink, Himalayan

Black Pepper, to taste

EQUIPMENT:

Small and Medium and large mixing bowls, Medium heat-proof pot, Large frying pan and/or Large baking tray, Measuring cups, Kitchen knife, Spatula.

DIRECTIONS:

Step 1: Place bread crumbs into a small mixing bowl and add warm milk. Mix well and leave on a countertop for ten to fifteen minutes.

Step 2: Place ground beef and ground pork into a medium mixing bowl. Mix it well and add soften bread crumbs and egg to the mixture.

Step 3: Add spices, salt, and pepper and mix well to incorporate.

Step 4: Make round shape balls and place onto a large tray. Make sure the sides of the meatballs do not touch to ensure even cooking.

You can bake meatballs in an oven or fry them in a pan.

Bake the meatballs in an oven:

Step 1: Preheat the oven to 360°F.

Step 2: Place the tray with meatballs into the oven. Bake until meatballs internal temperature gets to 165°F. This can take between 50 minutes and 1 hour and ten minutes.

Fry the meatballs in a pan.

Step 1: Spray a frying pan with a cooking spray and preheat the pan. You can get away with not using cooking spray because there will be enough fat released during frying.

Step 2: Place the meatballs into the frying pan. Make sure the sides of meatballs do not touch to ensure an even cooking.

Fry for about 30 minutes, flipping from side to side, until meatballs internal temperature gets to 165°F.

Serve immediately.

Chickpea Meatballs will keep for three days in a fridge or one month in a freezer.

Thank You for Purchasing This Book!

I create and test recipes for you. I hope you enjoyed these recipes.

Your review of this book helps me succeed & grow. If you enjoyed this book, please leave me a short (1-2 sentence) review on Amazon.

Thank you so much for reviewing this book!

Do you have any questions?
Email me at: **cookbooks@m-a-i-a.com and subscribe to our weekly free recipes. Please put "Recipes" in the subject.**

MARIA SOBININA
m-a-i-a.com & maiatea.com

Printed in Great Britain
by Amazon